MEOW-NIFICENT KITTENS

The Secret Personal Internet Address & Password Log Book for Kitten & Cat Lovers

Ceri Clark

MEOW-NIFICENT KITTENS: The Secret Personal Internet Address
& Password Log Book for Kitten & Cat Lovers

© 2016 Cover & Interior Design: Ceri Clark

First Edition
ISBN-10: 1-68063-037-7
ISBN-13: 978-1-68063-037-4
Published by
Myrddin Publishing Group
Contact us at - www.myrddinpublishing.com

unique electronic & print books

IMPORTANT, PLEASE READ

Are you always forgetting or losing your passwords? Are you worried about having a password organizer that screams "steal me" if you get burgled? Would you like a password book but you want something a little different?

If this sounds familiar, then this book was made for you. The cover is designed so it won't get noticed by thieves who are looking for an obvious password logbook. Of course it is also protected from online thieves by being a paperback! Simply slip this volume into your bookshelves with other books to hide it in plain sight.

There is a risk that if someone steals this or any other password keeper then they can get into your internet accounts. For this reason, please keep this book safe and secure and hidden at home.

To help you, this section shares tips for creating a secure password. This will make it difficult for anyone to get into your accounts even if they get this book.

First of all, your password needs to be strong. Whatever you choose, there should be at least 8 characters in your password. If possible, these should be a mixture of lower and uppercase letters, numbers and special characters such as a $, *, &, @ etc.

The secret to using this book with this tip is that you only write down half of the password in this book. What you record needs to be random with a combination of characters. The reason that this method is secure is that half of the password is (only) stored in your head. It does not matter where you put the memorized half of the password into the complete password. This can be at the beginning, middle or end, as long as it is not written

Example
Memorized half (only in your head):
wind
Recorded half (in spreadsheet):
Hydf54j@#f
Full password while logging in:
windHydf54j@#f

down and is consistent so you remember it. The box above shows how this can work in practice.

As you can see this would be difficult to guess. You should not store it in an online password vault service unless you put it behind something protected by 2-step authentication.

Other ways to write down your password could be to use a code or have a theme but these can be very difficult to remember or will involve so much time to work it out that you will end up writing the real password anyway. The advantage of the above method is that you only need to remember the one 'password', albeit half a password but every password will still be different.

2-step verification/authentication is an extra step to make sure that access to your information, files and folders on an online service is restricted to you. Instead of relying on a password (which might be gained through nefarious means by hackers from a website or other means), a second device is used which you always have on you such as a phone, tablet computer or key ring. Using the 2-step verification method along with a secure password would mean any would-be infiltrator, bent on your destruction would need to have your password from this book, the memorized word from your mind AND your phone to gain access to your account.

For an example of how to setup 2-step verification, please download my free e-book, A Simpler Guide to Online Security, available at all good online retailers (paperback also available) from:

http://cericlark.com/Ae

Site Name ....
Site Address ....
Username ....
Password ....
Email ....
Password hint ....
Pin ....
Notes ....
....

Site Name ....
Site Address ....
Username ....
Password ....
Email ....
Password hint ....
Pin ....
Notes ....
....

Site Name ....
Site Address ....
Username ....
Password ....
Email ....
Password hint ....
Pin ....
Notes ....
....

Site Name	....
Site Address	....
Username	....
Password	....
Email	....
Password hint	....
Pin	....
Notes	....
	....

Site Name	....
Site Address	....
Username	....
Password	....
Email	....
Password hint	....
Pin	....
Notes	....
	....

Site Name	....
Site Address	....
Username	....
Password	....
Email	....
Password hint	....
Pin	....
Notes	....
	....

A-B
C-D
E-F
G-H
I-J
K-L
M-N
O-P
Q-R
S-T
U-V
W-X
Y-Z

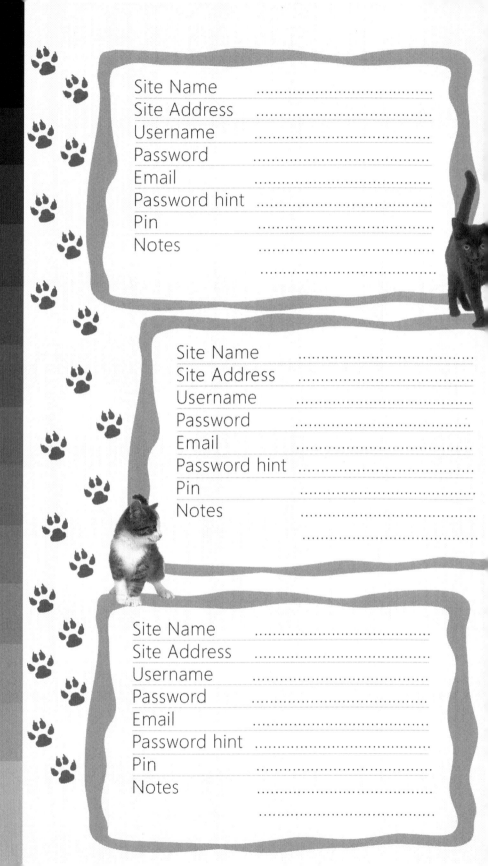

Site Name ....

Site Address ....

Username ....

Password ....

Email ....

Password hint ....

Pin ....

Notes ....

....

Site Name ....

Site Address ....

Username ....

Password ....

Email ....

Password hint ....

Pin ....

Notes ....

....

Site Name ....

Site Address ....

Username ....

Password ....

Email ....

Password hint ....

Pin ....

Notes ....

....

Site Name ....
Site Address ....
Username ....
Password ....
Email ....
Password hint ....
Pin ....
Notes ....
....

Site Name ....
Site Address ....
Username ....
Password ....
Email ....
Password hint ....
Pin ....
Notes ....
....

Site Name ....
Site Address ....
Username ....
Password ....
Email ....
Password hint ....
Pin ....
Notes ....
....

A-B

C-D

E-F

G-H

I-J

K-L

M-N

O-P

Q-R

S-T

U-V

W-X

Y-Z

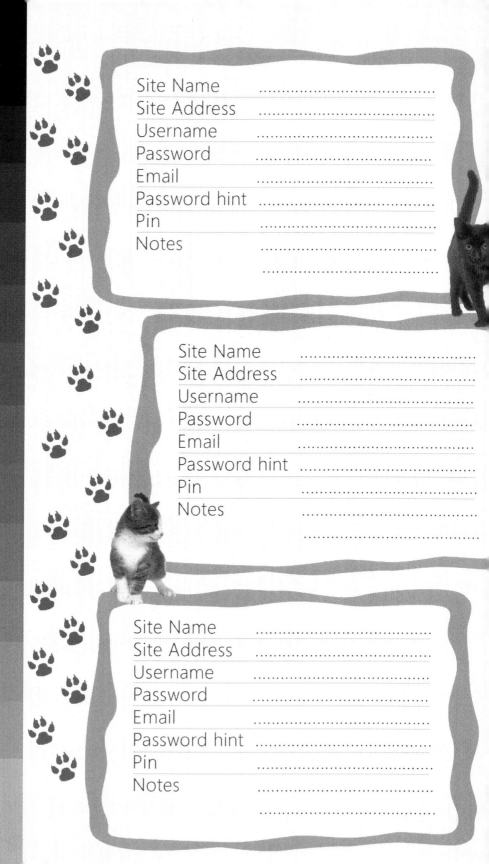

Site Name ....

Site Address ....

Username ....

Password ....

Email ....

Password hint ....

Pin ....

Notes ....

....

Site Name ....

Site Address ....

Username ....

Password ....

Email ....

Password hint ....

Pin ....

Notes ....

....

Site Name ....

Site Address ....

Username ....

Password ....

Email ....

Password hint ....

Pin ....

Notes ....

....

Site Name	....
Site Address	....
Username	....
Password	....
Email	....
Password hint	....
Pin	....
Notes	....
	....

Site Name	....
Site Address	....
Username	....
Password	....
Email	....
Password hint	....
Pin	....
Notes	....
	....

Site Name	....
Site Address	....
Username	....
Password	....
Email	....
Password hint	....
Pin	....
Notes	....
	....

Site Name ....
Site Address ....
Username ....
Password ....
Email ....
Password hint ....
Pin ....
Notes ....
....

Site Name ....
Site Address ....
Username ....
Password ....
Email ....
Password hint ....
Pin ....
Notes ....
....

Site Name ....
Site Address ....
Username ....
Password ....
Email ....
Password hint ....
Pin ....
Notes ....
....

Site Name	....
Site Address	....
Username	....
Password	....
Email	....
Password hint	....
Pin	....
Notes	....
	....

Site Name	....
Site Address	....
Username	....
Password	....
Email	....
Password hint	....
Pin	....
Notes	....
	....

Site Name	....
Site Address	....
Username	....
Password	....
Email	....
Password hint	....
Pin	....
Notes	....
	....

A-B

C-D

E-F

G-H

I-J

K-L

M-N

O-P

Q-R

S-T

U-V

W-X

Y-Z

Site Name ....
Site Address ....
Username ....
Password ....
Email ....
Password hint ....
Pin ....
Notes ....
....

Site Name ....
Site Address ....
Username ....
Password ....
Email ....
Password hint ....
Pin ....
Notes ....
....

Site Name ....
Site Address ....
Username ....
Password ....
Email ....
Password hint ....
Pin ....
Notes ....
....

Site Name	....
Site Address	....
Username	....
Password	....
Email	....
Password hint	....
Pin	....
Notes	....
	....

Site Name	....
Site Address	....
Username	....
Password	....
Email	....
Password hint	....
Pin	....
Notes	....
	....

Site Name	....
Site Address	....
Username	....
Password	....
Email	....
Password hint	....
Pin	....
Notes	....
	....

A-B

C-D

E-F

G-H

I-J

K-L

M-N

O-P

Q-R

S-T

U-V

W-X

Y-Z

Site Name   ....
Site Address   ....
Username   ....
Password   ....
Email   ....
Password hint   ....
Pin   ....
Notes   ....
                  ....

Site Name   ....
Site Address   ....
Username   ....
Password   ....
Email   ....
Password hint   ....
Pin   ....
Notes   ....
                  ....

Site Name   ....
Site Address   ....
Username   ....
Password   ....
Email   ....
Password hint   ....
Pin   ....
Notes   ....
                  ....

Site Name	....
Site Address	....
Username	....
Password	....
Email	....
Password hint	....
Pin	....
Notes	....
	....

Site Name	....
Site Address	....
Username	....
Password	....
Email	....
Password hint	....
Pin	....
Notes	....
	....

Site Name	....
Site Address	....
Username	....
Password	....
Email	....
Password hint	....
Pin	....
Notes	....
	....

A-B
C-D
E-F
G-H
I-J
K-L
M-N
O-P
Q-R
S-T
U-V
W-X
Y-Z

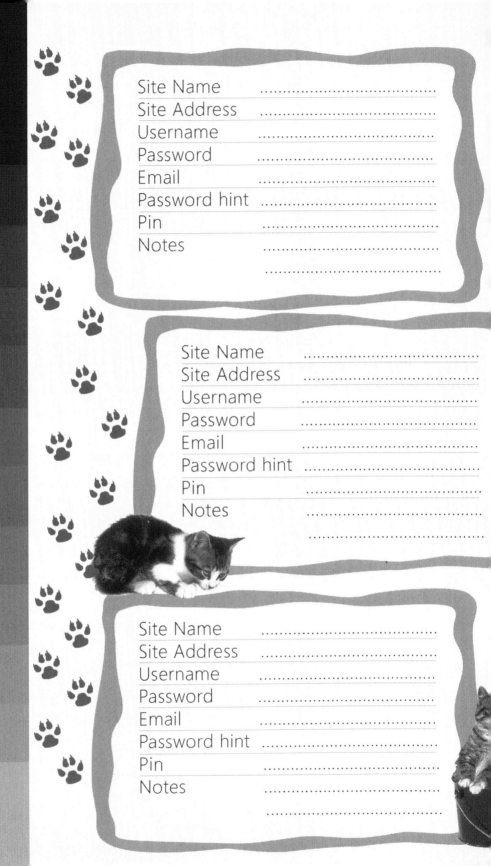

Site Name ....

Site Address ....

Username ....

Password ....

Email ....

Password hint ....

Pin ....

Notes ....

....

Site Name ....

Site Address ....

Username ....

Password ....

Email ....

Password hint ....

Pin ....

Notes ....

....

Site Name ....

Site Address ....

Username ....

Password ....

Email ....

Password hint ....

Pin ....

Notes ....

....

Site Name	....
Site Address	....
Username	....
Password	....
Email	....
Password hint	....
Pin	....
Notes	....
	....

Site Name	....
Site Address	....
Username	....
Password	....
Email	....
Password hint	....
Pin	....
Notes	....
	....

Site Name	....
Site Address	....
Username	....
Password	....
Email	....
Password hint	....
Pin	....
Notes	....
	....

C-D
E-F
G-H
I-J
K-L
M-N
O-P
Q-R
S-T
U-V
W-X
Y-Z

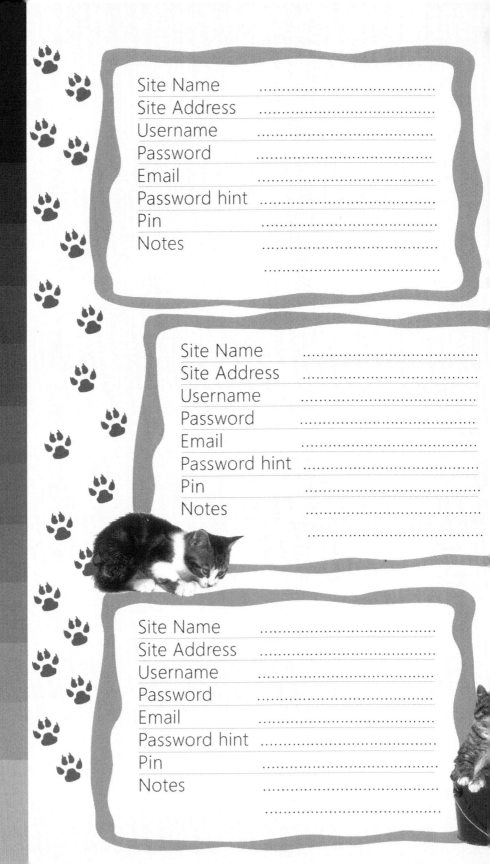

Site Name ....
Site Address ....
Username ....
Password ....
Email ....
Password hint ....
Pin ....
Notes ....
....

Site Name ....
Site Address ....
Username ....
Password ....
Email ....
Password hint ....
Pin ....
Notes ....
....

Site Name ....
Site Address ....
Username ....
Password ....
Email ....
Password hint ....
Pin ....
Notes ....
....

Site Name ....
Site Address ....
Username ....
Password ....
Email ....
Password hint ....
Pin ....
Notes ....
....

Site Name ....
Site Address ....
Username ....
Password ....
Email ....
Password hint ....
Pin ....
Notes ....
....

Site Name ....
Site Address ....
Username ....
Password ....
Email ....
Password hint ....
Pin ....
Notes ....
....

C-D

E-F

G-H

I-J

K-L

M-N

O-P

Q-R

S-T

U-V

W-X

Y-Z

Site Name ....

Site Address ....

Username ....

Password ....

Email ....

Password hint ....

Pin ....

Notes ....

....

Site Name ....

Site Address ....

Username ....

Password ....

Email ....

Password hint ....

Pin ....

Notes ....

....

Site Name ....

Site Address ....

Username ....

Password ....

Email ....

Password hint ....

Pin ....

Notes ....

....

Site Name ....
Site Address ....
Username ....
Password ....
Email ....
Password hint ....
Pin ....
Notes ....
....

Site Name ....
Site Address ....
Username ....
Password ....
Email ....
Password hint ....
Pin ....
Notes ....
....

Site Name ....
Site Address ....
Username ....
Password ....
Email ....
Password hint ....
Pin ....
Notes ....
....

C-D

E-F

G-H

I-J

K-L

M-N

O-P

Q-R

S-T

U-V

W-X

Y-Z

Site Name ....

Site Address ....

Username ....

Password ....

Email ....

Password hint ....

Pin ....

Notes ....

....

Site Name ....

Site Address ....

Username ....

Password ....

Email ....

Password hint ....

Pin ....

Notes ....

....

Site Name ....

Site Address ....

Username ....

Password ....

Email ....

Password hint ....

Pin ....

Notes ....

....

Site Name ....
Site Address ....
Username ....
Password ....
Email ....
Password hint ....
Pin ....
Notes ....
....

Site Name ....
Site Address ....
Username ....
Password ....
Email ....
Password hint ....
Pin ....
Notes ....
....

Site Name ....
Site Address ....
Username ....
Password ....
Email ....
Password hint ....
Pin ....
Notes ....
....

C-D

E-F

G-H

I-J

K-L

M-N

O-P

Q-R

S-T

U-V

W-X

Y-Z

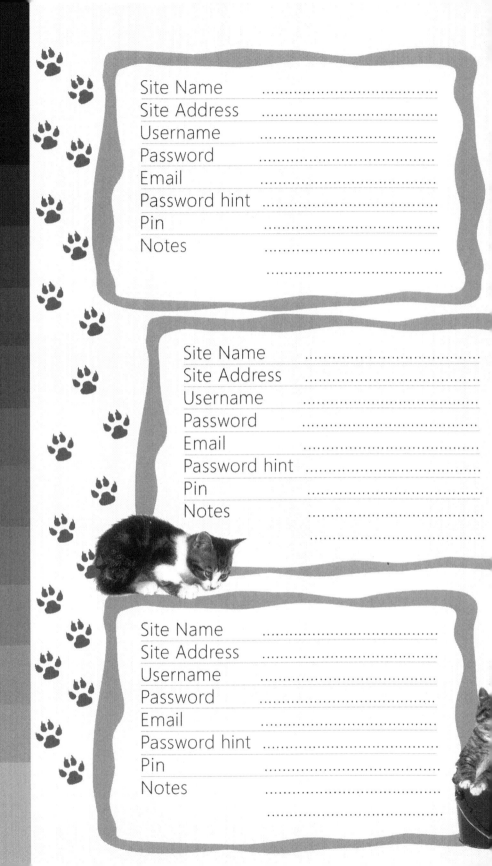

Site Name   ....

Site Address   ....

Username   ....

Password   ....

Email   ....

Password hint ....

Pin   ....

Notes   ....

     ....

Site Name   ....

Site Address   ....

Username   ....

Password   ....

Email   ....

Password hint ....

Pin   ....

Notes   ....

     ....

Site Name   ....

Site Address   ....

Username   ....

Password   ....

Email   ....

Password hint ....

Pin   ....

Notes   ....

     ....

Site Name ....
Site Address ....
Username ....
Password ....
Email ....
Password hint ....
Pin ....
Notes ....
....

Site Name ....
Site Address ....
Username ....
Password ....
Email ....
Password hint ....
Pin ....
Notes ....
....

Site Name ....
Site Address ....
Username ....
Password ....
Email ....
Password hint ....
Pin ....
Notes ....
....

E-F
G-H
I-J
K-L
M-N
O-P
Q-R
S-T
U-V
W-X
Y-Z

Site Name ....
Site Address ....
Username ....
Password ....
Email ....
Password hint ....
Pin ....
Notes ....
....

Site Name ....
Site Address ....
Username ....
Password ....
Email ....
Password hint ....
Pin ....
Notes ....
....

Site Name ....
Site Address ....
Username ....
Password ....
Email ....
Password hint ....
Pin ....
Notes ....
....

Site Name ....
Site Address ....
Username ....
Password ....
Email ....
Password hint ....
Pin ....
Notes ....
....

Site Name ....
Site Address ....
Username ....
Password ....
Email ....
Password hint ....
Pin ....
Notes ....
....

Site Name ....
Site Address ....
Username ....
Password ....
Email ....
Password hint ....
Pin ....
Notes ....
....

E-F

G-H

I-J

K-L

M-N

O-P

Q-R

S-T

U-V

W-X

Y-Z

Site Name ....

Site Address ....

Username ....

Password ....

Email ....

Password hint ....

Pin ....

Notes ....

....

Site Name ....

Site Address ....

Username ....

Password ....

Email ....

Password hint ....

Pin ....

Notes ....

....

Site Name ....

Site Address ....

Username ....

Password ....

Email ....

Password hint ....

Pin ....

Notes ....

....

Site Name ....
Site Address ....
Username ....
Password ....
Email ....
Password hint ....
Pin ....
Notes ....
....

Site Name ....
Site Address ....
Username ....
Password ....
Email ....
Password hint ....
Pin ....
Notes ....
....

Site Name ....
Site Address ....
Username ....
Password ....
Email ....
Password hint ....
Pin ....
Notes ....
....

E-F
G-H
I-J
K-L
M-N
O-P
Q-R
S-T
U-V
W-X
Y-Z

Site Name ....
Site Address ....
Username ....
Password ....
Email ....
Password hint ....
Pin ....
Notes ....
....

Site Name ....
Site Address ....
Username ....
Password ....
Email ....
Password hint ....
Pin ....
Notes ....
....

Site Name ....
Site Address ....
Username ....
Password ....
Email ....
Password hint ....
Pin ....
Notes ....
....

Site Name ....
Site Address ....
Username ....
Password ....
Email ....
Password hint ....
Pin ....
Notes ....
....

Site Name ....
Site Address ....
Username ....
Password ....
Email ....
Password hint ....
Pin ....
Notes ....
....

Site Name ....
Site Address ....
Username ....
Password ....
Email ....
Password hint ....
Pin ....
Notes ....
....

E-F

G-H

I-J

K-L

M-N

O-P

Q-R

S-T

U-V

W-X

Y-Z

Site Name ....

Site Address ....

Username ....

Password ....

Email ....

Password hint ....

Pin ....

Notes ....

....

Site Name ....

Site Address ....

Username ....

Password ....

Email ....

Password hint ....

Pin ....

Notes ....

....

Site Name ....

Site Address ....

Username ....

Password ....

Email ....

Password hint ....

Pin ....

Notes ....

....

Site Name ....
Site Address ....
Username ....
Password ....
Email ....
Password hint ....
Pin ....
Notes ....
....

Site Name ....
Site Address ....
Username ....
Password ....
Email ....
Password hint ....
Pin ....
Notes ....
....

Site Name ....
Site Address ....
Username ....
Password ....
Email ....
Password hint ....
Pin ....
Notes ....
....

E-F

G-H

I-J

K-L

M-N

O-P

Q-R

S-T

U-V

W-X

Y-Z

Site Name ....

Site Address ....

Username ....

Password ....

Email ....

Password hint ....

Pin ....

Notes ....

....

Site Name ....

Site Address ....

Username ....

Password ....

Email ....

Password hint ....

Pin ....

Notes ....

....

Site Name ....

Site Address ....

Username ....

Password ....

Email ....

Password hint ....

Pin ....

Notes ....

....

Site Name ....

Site Address ....

Username ....

Password ....

Email ....

Password hint ....

Pin ....

Notes ....

....

Site Name ....

Site Address ....

Username ....

Password ....

Email ....

Password hint ....

Pin ....

Notes ....

....

Site Name ....

Site Address ....

Username ....

Password ....

Email ....

Password hint ....

Pin ....

Notes ....

....

G-H

I-J

K-L

M-N

O-P

Q-R

S-T

U-V

W-X

Y-Z

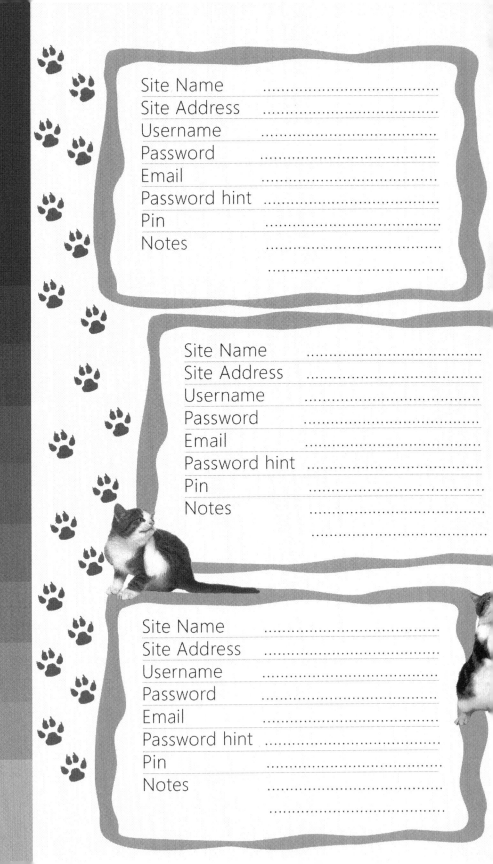

Site Name ....
Site Address ....
Username ....
Password ....
Email ....
Password hint ....
Pin ....
Notes ....
....

Site Name ....
Site Address ....
Username ....
Password ....
Email ....
Password hint ....
Pin ....
Notes ....
....

Site Name ....
Site Address ....
Username ....
Password ....
Email ....
Password hint ....
Pin ....
Notes ....
....

Site Name ....
Site Address ....
Username ....
Password ....
Email ....
Password hint ....
Pin ....
Notes ....
....

Site Name ....
Site Address ....
Username ....
Password ....
Email ....
Password hint ....
Pin ....
Notes ....
....

Site Name ....
Site Address ....
Username ....
Password ....
Email ....
Password hint ....
Pin ....
Notes ....
....

G-H

I-J

K-L

M-N

O-P

Q-R

S-T

U-V

W-X

Y-Z

Site Name ....

Site Address ....

Username ....

Password ....

Email ....

Password hint ....

Pin ....

Notes ....

....

Site Name ....

Site Address ....

Username ....

Password ....

Email ....

Password hint ....

Pin ....

Notes ....

....

Site Name ....

Site Address ....

Username ....

Password ....

Email ....

Password hint ....

Pin ....

Notes ....

....

Site Name ....

Site Address ....

Username ....

Password ....

Email ....

Password hint ....

Pin ....

Notes ....

....

Site Name ....

Site Address ....

Username ....

Password ....

Email ....

Password hint ....

Pin ....

Notes ....

....

Site Name ....

Site Address ....

Username ....

Password ....

Email ....

Password hint ....

Pin ....

Notes ....

....

G-H

I-J

K-L

M-N

O-P

Q-R

S-T

U-V

W-X

Y-Z

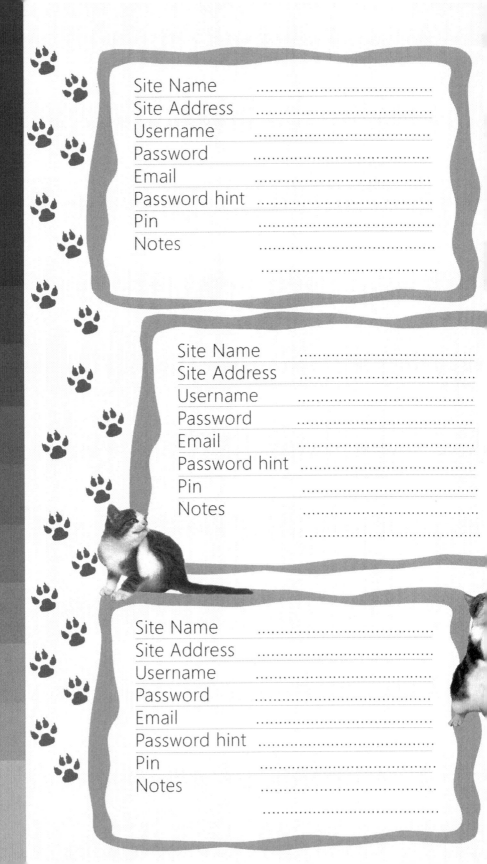

Site Name ....

Site Address ....

Username ....

Password ....

Email ....

Password hint ....

Pin ....

Notes ....

....

Site Name ....

Site Address ....

Username ....

Password ....

Email ....

Password hint ....

Pin ....

Notes ....

....

Site Name ....

Site Address ....

Username ....

Password ....

Email ....

Password hint ....

Pin ....

Notes ....

....

Site Name ....
Site Address ....
Username ....
Password ....
Email ....
Password hint ....
Pin ....
Notes ....
....

Site Name ....
Site Address ....
Username ....
Password ....
Email ....
Password hint ....
Pin ....
Notes ....
....

Site Name ....
Site Address ....
Username ....
Password ....
Email ....
Password hint ....
Pin ....
Notes ....
....

G-H

I-J

K-L

M-N

O-P

Q-R

S-T

U-V

W-X

Y-Z

Site Name ....

Site Address ....

Username ....

Password ....

Email ....

Password hint ....

Pin ....

Notes ....

....

Site Name ....

Site Address ....

Username ....

Password ....

Email ....

Password hint ....

Pin ....

Notes ....

....

Site Name ....

Site Address ....

Username ....

Password ....

Email ....

Password hint ....

Pin ....

Notes ....

....

Site Name ....

Site Address ....

Username ....

Password ....

Email ....

Password hint ....

Pin ....

Notes ....

....

Site Name ....

Site Address ....

Username ....

Password ....

Email ....

Password hint ....

Pin ....

Notes ....

....

Site Name ....

Site Address ....

Username ....

Password ....

Email ....

Password hint ....

Pin ....

Notes ....

....

G-H

I-J

K-L

M-N

O-P

Q-R

S-T

U-V

W-X

Y-Z

Site Name ....

Site Address ....

Username ....

Password ....

Email ....

Password hint ....

Pin ....

Notes ....

....

Site Name ....

Site Address ....

Username ....

Password ....

Email ....

Password hint ....

Pin ....

Notes ....

....

Site Name ....

Site Address ....

Username ....

Password ....

Email ....

Password hint ....

Pin ....

Notes ....

....

Site Name ....

Site Address ....

Username ....

Password ....

Email ....

Password hint ....

Pin ....

Notes ....

....

Site Name ....

Site Address ....

Username ....

Password ....

Email ....

Password hint ....

Pin ....

Notes ....

....

Site Name ....

Site Address ....

Username ....

Password ....

Email ....

Password hint ....

Pin ....

Notes ....

....

G-H

I-J

K-L

M-N

O-P

Q-R

S-T

U-V

W-X

Y-Z

Site Name ....
Site Address ....
Username ....
Password ....
Email ....
Password hint ....
Pin ....
Notes ....
....

Site Name ....
Site Address ....
Username ....
Password ....
Email ....
Password hint ....
Pin ....
Notes ....
....

Site Name ....
Site Address ....
Username ....
Password ....
Email ....
Password hint ....
Pin ....
Notes ....
....

Site Name ....
Site Address ....
Username ....
Password ....
Email ....
Password hint ....
Pin ....
Notes ....
....

Site Name ....
Site Address ....
Username ....
Password ....
Email ....
Password hint ....
Pin ....
Notes ....
....

Site Name ....
Site Address ....
Username ....
Password ....
Email ....
Password hint ....
Pin ....
Notes ....
....

I-J

K-L

M-N

O-P

Q-R

S-T

U-V

W-X

Y-Z

Site Name ....

Site Address ....

Username ....

Password ....

Email ....

Password hint ....

Pin ....

Notes ....

....

Site Name ....

Site Address ....

Username ....

Password ....

Email ....

Password hint ....

Pin ....

Notes ....

....

Site Name ....

Site Address ....

Username ....

Password ....

Email ....

Password hint ....

Pin ....

Notes ....

....

Site Name ....
Site Address ....
Username ....
Password ....
Email ....
Password hint ....
Pin ....
Notes ....
....

Site Name ....
Site Address ....
Username ....
Password ....
Email ....
Password hint ....
Pin ....
Notes ....
....

Site Name ....
Site Address ....
Username ....
Password ....
Email ....
Password hint ....
Pin ....
Notes ....
....

I-J

K-L

M-N

O-P

Q-R

S-T

U-V

W-X

Y-Z

Site Name ....

Site Address ....

Username ....

Password ....

Email ....

Password hint ....

Pin ....

Notes ....

....

Site Name ....

Site Address ....

Username ....

Password ....

Email ....

Password hint ....

Pin ....

Notes ....

....

Site Name ....

Site Address ....

Username ....

Password ....

Email ....

Password hint ....

Pin ....

Notes ....

....

Site Name ....

Site Address ....

Username ....

Password ....

Email ....

Password hint ....

Pin ....

Notes ....

....

Site Name ....

Site Address ....

Username ....

Password ....

Email ....

Password hint ....

Pin ....

Notes ....

....

Site Name ....

Site Address ....

Username ....

Password ....

Email ....

Password hint ....

Pin ....

Notes ....

....

I-J

K-L

M-N

O-P

Q-R

S-T

U-V

W-X

Y-Z

Site Name	....
Site Address	....
Username	....
Password	....
Email	....
Password hint	....
Pin	....
Notes	....
	....

Site Name	....
Site Address	....
Username	....
Password	....
Email	....
Password hint	....
Pin	....
Notes	....
	....

Site Name	....
Site Address	....
Username	....
Password	....
Email	....
Password hint	....
Pin	....
Notes	....
	....

Site Name   ....
Site Address ....
Username   ....
Password   ....
Email   ....
Password hint ....
Pin   ....
Notes   ....
             ....

Site Name   ....
Site Address ....
Username   ....
Password   ....
Email   ....
Password hint ....
Pin   ....
Notes   ....
             ....

Site Name   ....
Site Address ....
Username   ....
Password   ....
Email   ....
Password hint ....
Pin   ....
Notes   ....
             ....

I-J

K-L

M-N

O-P

Q-R

S-T

U-V

W-X

Y-Z

Site Name ....

Site Address ....

Username ....

Password ....

Email ....

Password hint ....

Pin ....

Notes ....

....

Site Name ....

Site Address ....

Username ....

Password ....

Email ....

Password hint ....

Pin ....

Notes ....

....

Site Name ....

Site Address ....

Username ....

Password ....

Email ....

Password hint ....

Pin ....

Notes ....

....

Site Name ....
Site Address ....
Username ....
Password ....
Email ....
Password hint ....
Pin ....
Notes ....
....

Site Name ....
Site Address ....
Username ....
Password ....
Email ....
Password hint ....
Pin ....
Notes ....
....

Site Name ....
Site Address ....
Username ....
Password ....
Email ....
Password hint ....
Pin ....
Notes ....
....

I-J

K-L

M-N

O-P

Q-R

S-T

U-V

W-X

Y-Z

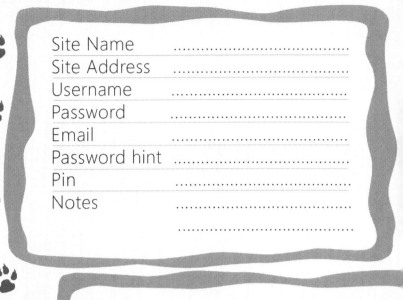

Site Name ....
Site Address ....
Username ....
Password ....
Email ....
Password hint ....
Pin ....
Notes ....
....

Site Name ....
Site Address ....
Username ....
Password ....
Email ....
Password hint ....
Pin ....
Notes ....
....

Site Name ....
Site Address ....
Username ....
Password ....
Email ....
Password hint ....
Pin ....
Notes ....
....

Site Name	....
Site Address	....
Username	....
Password	....
Email	....
Password hint	....
Pin	....
Notes	....
	....

Site Name	....
Site Address	....
Username	....
Password	....
Email	....
Password hint	....
Pin	....
Notes	....
	....

Site Name	....
Site Address	....
Username	....
Password	....
Email	....
Password hint	....
Pin	....
Notes	....
	....

K-L

M-N

O-P

Q-R

S-T

U-V

W-X

Y-Z

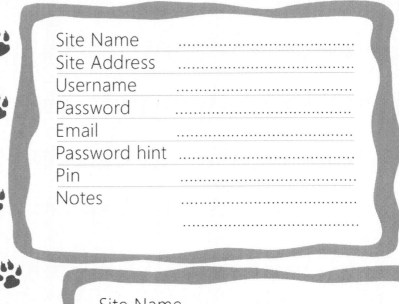

Site Name ....

Site Address ....

Username ....

Password ....

Email ....

Password hint ....

Pin ....

Notes ....

....

Site Name ....

Site Address ....

Username ....

Password ....

Email ....

Password hint ....

Pin ....

Notes ....

....

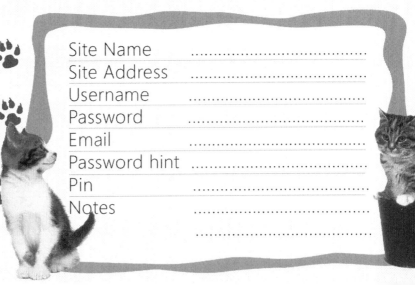

Site Name ....

Site Address ....

Username ....

Password ....

Email ....

Password hint ....

Pin ....

Notes ....

....

Site Name ....
Site Address ....
Username ....
Password ....
Email ....
Password hint ....
Pin ....
Notes ....
....

Site Name ....
Site Address ....
Username ....
Password ....
Email ....
Password hint ....
Pin ....
Notes ....
....

Site Name ....
Site Address ....
Username ....
Password ....
Email ....
Password hint ....
Pin ....
Notes ....
....

K-L

M-N

O-P

Q-R

S-T

U-V

W-X

Y-Z

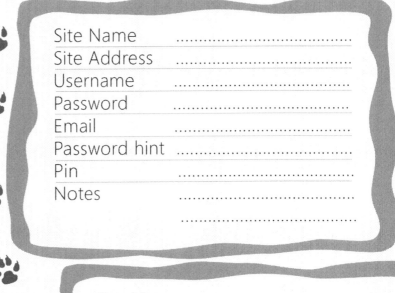

Site Name   ....
Site Address   ....
Username   ....
Password   ....
Email   ....
Password hint   ....
Pin   ....
Notes   ....
                 ....

Site Name   ....
Site Address   ....
Username   ....
Password   ....
Email   ....
Password hint   ....
Pin   ....
Notes   ....
                 ....

Site Name   ....
Site Address   ....
Username   ....
Password   ....
Email   ....
Password hint   ....
Pin   ....
Notes   ....
                 ....

Site Name ....
Site Address ....
Username ....
Password ....
Email ....
Password hint ....
Pin ....
Notes ....
....

Site Name ....
Site Address ....
Username ....
Password ....
Email ....
Password hint ....
Pin ....
Notes ....
....

Site Name ....
Site Address ....
Username ....
Password ....
Email ....
Password hint ....
Pin ....
Notes ....
....

K-L

M-N

O-P

Q-R

S-T

U-V

W-X

Y-Z

Site Name	....
Site Address	....
Username	....
Password	....
Email	....
Password hint	....
Pin	....
Notes	....
	....

Site Name	....
Site Address	....
Username	....
Password	....
Email	....
Password hint	....
Pin	....
Notes	....
	....

Site Name	....
Site Address	....
Username	....
Password	....
Email	....
Password hint	....
Pin	....
Notes	....
	....

Site Name	....
Site Address	....
Username	....
Password	....
Email	....
Password hint	....
Pin	....
Notes	....
	....

Site Name	....
Site Address	....
Username	....
Password	....
Email	....
Password hint	....
Pin	....
Notes	....
	....

K-L

M-N

O-P

Q-R

S-T

U-V

W-X

Y-Z

Site Name	....
Site Address	....
Username	....
Password	....
Email	....
Password hint	....
Pin	....
Notes	....
	....

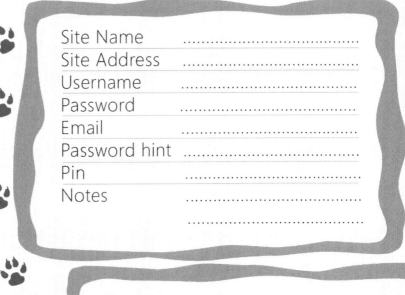

Site Name   ....
Site Address ....
Username   ....
Password   ....
Email   ....
Password hint ....
Pin   ....
Notes   ....
           ....

Site Name   ....
Site Address ....
Username   ....
Password   ....
Email   ....
Password hint ....
Pin   ....
Notes   ....
           ....

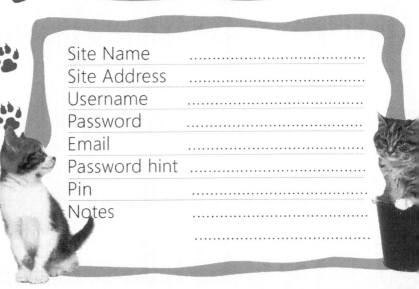

Site Name   ....
Site Address ....
Username   ....
Password   ....
Email   ....
Password hint ....
Pin   ....
Notes   ....
           ....

Site Name ....
Site Address ....
Username ....
Password ....
Email ....
Password hint ....
Pin ....
Notes ....
....

Site Name ....
Site Address ....
Username ....
Password ....
Email ....
Password hint ....
Pin ....
Notes ....
....

Site Name ....
Site Address ....
Username ....
Password ....
Email ....
Password hint ....
Pin ....
Notes ....
....

K-L

M-N

O-P

Q-R

S-T

U-V

W-X

Y-Z

Site Name ....
Site Address ....
Username ....
Password ....
Email ....
Password hint ....
Pin ....
Notes ....
....

Site Name ....
Site Address ....
Username ....
Password ....
Email ....
Password hint ....
Pin ....
Notes ....
....

Site Name ....
Site Address ....
Username ....
Password ....
Email ....
Password hint ....
Pin ....
Notes ....
....

Site Name	....
Site Address	....
Username	....
Password	....
Email	....
Password hint	....
Pin	....
Notes	....
	....

Site Name	....
Site Address	....
Username	....
Password	....
Email	....
Password hint	....
Pin	....
Notes	....
	....

Site Name	....
Site Address	....
Username	....
Password	....
Email	....
Password hint	....
Pin	....
Notes	....
	....

M-N

O-P

Q-R

S-T

U-V

W-X

Y-Z

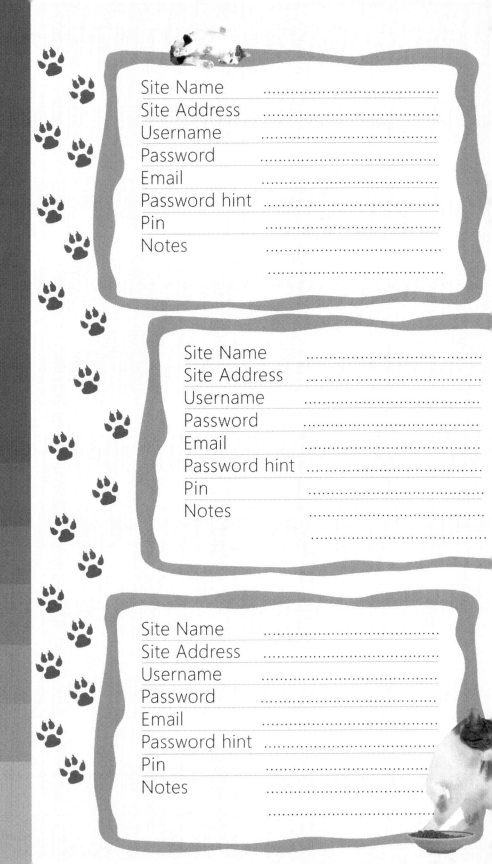

Site Name   ....
Site Address   ....
Username   ....
Password   ....
Email   ....
Password hint   ....
Pin   ....
Notes   ....
                   ....

Site Name   ....
Site Address   ....
Username   ....
Password   ....
Email   ....
Password hint   ....
Pin   ....
Notes   ....
                   ....

Site Name   ....
Site Address   ....
Username   ....
Password   ....
Email   ....
Password hint   ....
Pin   ....
Notes   ....
                   ....

Site Name	....
Site Address	....
Username	....
Password	....
Email	....
Password hint	....
Pin	....
Notes	....
	....

Site Name	....
Site Address	....
Username	....
Password	....
Email	....
Password hint	....
Pin	....
Notes	....
	....

M-N

O-P

Q-R

S-T

U-V

W-X

Y-Z

Site Name	....
Site Address	....
Username	....
Password	....
Email	....
Password hint	....
Pin	....
Notes	....
	....

Site Name ....

Site Address ....

Username ....

Password ....

Email ....

Password hint ....

Pin ....

Notes ....

....

Site Name ....

Site Address ....

Username ....

Password ....

Email ....

Password hint ....

Pin ....

Notes ....

....

Site Name ....

Site Address ....

Username ....

Password ....

Email ....

Password hint ....

Pin ....

Notes ....

....

Site Name ....
Site Address ....
Username ....
Password ....
Email ....
Password hint ....
Pin ....
Notes ....
....

Site Name ....
Site Address ....
Username ....
Password ....
Email ....
Password hint ....
Pin ....
Notes ....
....

M-N

O-P

Q-R

S-T

Site Name ....
Site Address ....
Username ....
Password ....
Email ....
Password hint ....
Pin ....
Notes ....
....

U-V

W-X

Y-Z

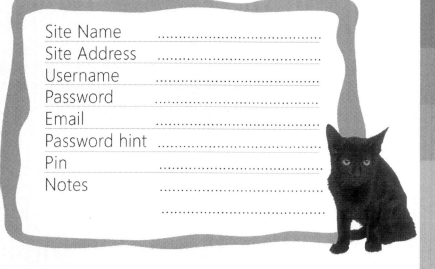

Site Name ....

Site Address ....

Username ....

Password ....

Email ....

Password hint ....

Pin ....

Notes ....

....

Site Name ....

Site Address ....

Username ....

Password ....

Email ....

Password hint ....

Pin ....

Notes ....

....

Site Name ....

Site Address ....

Username ....

Password ....

Email ....

Password hint ....

Pin ....

Notes ....

....

Site Name	....
Site Address	....
Username	....
Password	....
Email	....
Password hint	....
Pin	....
Notes	....
	....

Site Name	....
Site Address	....
Username	....
Password	....
Email	....
Password hint	....
Pin	....
Notes	....
	....

M-N

O-P

Q-R

S-T

U-V

W-X

Y-Z

Site Name	....
Site Address	....
Username	....
Password	....
Email	....
Password hint	....
Pin	....
Notes	....
	....

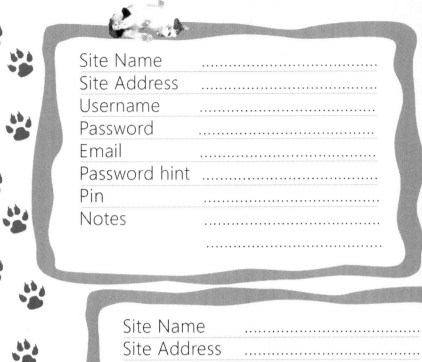

Site Name ....

Site Address ....

Username ....

Password ....

Email ....

Password hint ....

Pin ....

Notes ....

....

Site Name ....

Site Address ....

Username ....

Password ....

Email ....

Password hint ....

Pin ....

Notes ....

....

Site Name ....

Site Address ....

Username ....

Password ....

Email ....

Password hint ....

Pin ....

Notes ....

....

Site Name	....
Site Address	....
Username	....
Password	....
Email	....
Password hint	....
Pin	....
Notes	....
	....

Site Name	....
Site Address	....
Username	....
Password	....
Email	....
Password hint	....
Pin	....
Notes	....
	....

M-N

O-P

Q-R

S-T

U-V

W-X

Y-Z

Site Name	....
Site Address	....
Username	....
Password	....
Email	....
Password hint	....
Pin	....
Notes	....
	....

Site Name ....

Site Address ....

Username ....

Password ....

Email ....

Password hint ....

Pin ....

Notes ....

....

Site Name ....

Site Address ....

Username ....

Password ....

Email ....

Password hint ....

Pin ....

Notes ....

....

Site Name ....

Site Address ....

Username ....

Password ....

Email ....

Password hint ....

Pin ....

Notes ....

....

Site Name ....

Site Address ....

Username ....

Password ....

Email ....

Password hint ....

Pin ....

Notes ....

....

Site Name ....

Site Address ....

Username ....

Password ....

Email ....

Password hint ....

Pin ....

Notes ....

....

O-P

Q-R

S-T

Site Name ....

Site Address ....

Username ....

Password ....

Email ....

Password hint ....

Pin ....

Notes ....

....

U-V

W-X

Y-Z

Site Name ....
Site Address ....
Username ....
Password ....
Email ....
Password hint ....
Pin ....
Notes ....
....

Site Name ....
Site Address ....
Username ....
Password ....
Email ....
Password hint ....
Pin ....
Notes ....
....

Site Name ....
Site Address ....
Username ....
Password ....
Email ....
Password hint ....
Pin ....
Notes ....
....

Site Name ....
Site Address ....
Username ....
Password ....
Email ....
Password hint ....
Pin ....
Notes ....
....

Site Name ....
Site Address ....
Username ....
Password ....
Email ....
Password hint ....
Pin ....
Notes ....
....

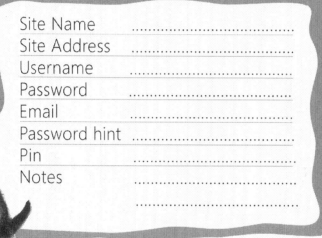

O-P

Q-R

S-T

Site Name ....
Site Address ....
Username ....
Password ....
Email ....
Password hint ....
Pin ....
Notes ....
....

U-V

W-X

Y-Z

Site Name ....
Site Address ....
Username ....
Password ....
Email ....
Password hint ....
Pin ....
Notes ....
....

Site Name ....
Site Address ....
Username ....
Password ....
Email ....
Password hint ....
Pin ....
Notes ....
....

Site Name ....
Site Address ....
Username ....
Password ....
Email ....
Password hint ....
Pin ....
Notes ....
....

Site Name ....
Site Address ....
Username ....
Password ....
Email ....
Password hint ....
Pin ....
Notes ....
....

Site Name ....
Site Address ....
Username ....
Password ....
Email ....
Password hint ....
Pin ....
Notes ....
....

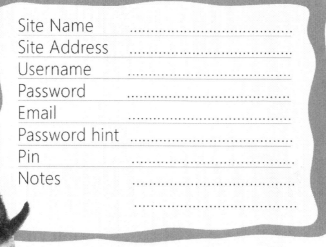

Site Name ....
Site Address ....
Username ....
Password ....
Email ....
Password hint ....
Pin ....
Notes ....
....

O-P

Q-R

S-T

U-V

W-X

Y-Z

Site Name	....
Site Address	....
Username	....
Password	....
Email	....
Password hint	....
Pin	....
Notes	....
	....

Site Name	....
Site Address	....
Username	....
Password	....
Email	....
Password hint	....
Pin	....
Notes	....
	....

Site Name	....
Site Address	....
Username	....
Password	....
Email	....
Password hint	....
Pin	....
Notes	....
	....

Site Name ....
Site Address ....
Username ....
Password ....
Email ....
Password hint ....
Pin ....
Notes ....
....

Site Name ....
Site Address ....
Username ....
Password ....
Email ....
Password hint ....
Pin ....
Notes ....
....

Site Name ....
Site Address ....
Username ....
Password ....
Email ....
Password hint ....
Pin ....
Notes ....
....

O-P

Q-R

S-T

U-V

W-X

Y-Z

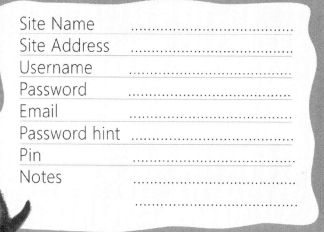

Site Name	....
Site Address	....
Username	....
Password	....
Email	....
Password hint	....
Pin	....
Notes	....
	....

Site Name	....
Site Address	....
Username	....
Password	....
Email	....
Password hint	....
Pin	....
Notes	....
	....

Site Name	....
Site Address	....
Username	....
Password	....
Email	....
Password hint	....
Pin	....
Notes	....
	....

Site Name   ....

Site Address   ....

Username   ....

Password   ....

Email   ....

Password hint   ....

Pin   ....

Notes   ....

....

Site Name   ....

Site Address   ....

Username   ....

Password   ....

Email   ....

Password hint   ....

Pin   ....

Notes   ....

....

Site Name   ....

Site Address   ....

Username   ....

Password   ....

Email   ....

Password hint   ....

Pin   ....

Notes   ....

....

Q-R

S-T

U-V

W-X

Y-Z

Site Name ....
Site Address ....
Username ....
Password ....
Email ....
Password hint ....
Pin ....
Notes ....
....

Site Name ....
Site Address ....
Username ....
Password ....
Email ....
Password hint ....
Pin ....
Notes ....
....

Site Name ....
Site Address ....
Username ....
Password ....
Email ....
Password hint ....
Pin ....
Notes ....
....

Site Name ....
Site Address ....
Username ....
Password ....
Email ....
Password hint ....
Pin ....
Notes ....
....

Site Name ....
Site Address ....
Username ....
Password ....
Email ....
Password hint ....
Pin ....
Notes ....
....

Site Name ....
Site Address ....
Username ....
Password ....
Email ....
Password hint ....
Pin ....
Notes ....
....

Q-R

S-T

U-V

W-X

Y-Z

Site Name ....

Site Address ....

Username ....

Password ....

Email ....

Password hint ....

Pin ....

Notes ....

....

Site Name ....

Site Address ....

Username ....

Password ....

Email ....

Password hint ....

Pin ....

Notes ....

....

Site Name ....

Site Address ....

Username ....

Password ....

Email ....

Password hint ....

Pin ....

Notes ....

....

Site Name ....
Site Address ....
Username ....
Password ....
Email ....
Password hint ....
Pin ....
Notes ....
....

Site Name ....
Site Address ....
Username ....
Password ....
Email ....
Password hint ....
Pin ....
Notes ....
....

Site Name ....
Site Address ....
Username ....
Password ....
Email ....
Password hint ....
Pin ....
Notes ....
....

Q-R

S-T

U-V

W-X

Y-Z

Site Name	....
Site Address	....
Username	....
Password	....
Email	....
Password hint	....
Pin	....
Notes	....
	....

Site Name	....
Site Address	....
Username	....
Password	....
Email	....
Password hint	....
Pin	....
Notes	....
	....

Site Name	....
Site Address	....
Username	....
Password	....
Email	....
Password hint	....
Pin	....
Notes	....
	....

Site Name ....
Site Address ....
Username ....
Password ....
Email ....
Password hint ....
Pin ....
Notes ....
....

Site Name ....
Site Address ....
Username ....
Password ....
Email ....
Password hint ....
Pin ....
Notes ....
....

Site Name ....
Site Address ....
Username ....
Password ....
Email ....
Password hint ....
Pin ....
Notes ....
....

Q-R

S-T

U-V

W-X

Y-Z

Site Name ....
Site Address ....
Username ....
Password ....
Email ....
Password hint ....
Pin ....
Notes ....
....

Site Name ....
Site Address ....
Username ....
Password ....
Email ....
Password hint ....
Pin ....
Notes ....
....

Site Name ....
Site Address ....
Username ....
Password ....
Email ....
Password hint ....
Pin ....
Notes ....
....

Site Name ....
Site Address ....
Username ....
Password ....
Email ....
Password hint ....
Pin ....
Notes ....
....

Site Name ....
Site Address ....
Username ....
Password ....
Email ....
Password hint ....
Pin ....
Notes ....
....

Site Name ....
Site Address ....
Username ....
Password ....
Email ....
Password hint ....
Pin ....
Notes ....
....

Q-R

S-T

U-V

W-X

Y-Z

Site Name	....
Site Address	....
Username	....
Password	....
Email	....
Password hint	....
Pin	....
Notes	....
	....

Site Name	....
Site Address	....
Username	....
Password	....
Email	....
Password hint	....
Pin	....
Notes	....
	....

Site Name	....
Site Address	....
Username	....
Password	....
Email	....
Password hint	....
Pin	....
Notes	....
	....

Site Name ....
Site Address ....
Username ....
Password ....
Email ....
Password hint ....
Pin ....
Notes ....
....

Site Name ....
Site Address ....
Username ....
Password ....
Email ....
Password hint ....
Pin ....
Notes ....
....

Site Name ....
Site Address ....
Username ....
Password ....
Email ....
Password hint ....
Pin ....
Notes ....
....

Q-R

S-T

U-V

W-X

Y-Z

Site Name ....

Site Address ....

Username ....

Password ....

Email ....

Password hint ....

Pin ....

Notes ....

....

Site Name ....

Site Address ....

Username ....

Password ....

Email ....

Password hint ....

Pin ....

Notes ....

....

Site Name ....

Site Address ....

Username ....

Password ....

Email ....

Password hint ....

Pin ....

Notes ....

....

Site Name ....
Site Address ....
Username ....
Password ....
Email ....
Password hint ....
Pin ....
Notes ....
....

Site Name ....
Site Address ....
Username ....
Password ....
Email ....
Password hint ....
Pin ....
Notes ....
....

Site Name ....
Site Address ....
Username ....
Password ....
Email ....
Password hint ....
Pin ....
Notes ....
....

S-T

U-V

W-X

Y-Z

Site Name ....
Site Address ....
Username ....
Password ....
Email ....
Password hint ....
Pin ....
Notes ....
....

Site Name ....
Site Address ....
Username ....
Password ....
Email ....
Password hint ....
Pin ....
Notes ....
....

Site Name ....
Site Address ....
Username ....
Password ....
Email ....
Password hint ....
Pin ....
Notes ....
....

Site Name ....

Site Address ....

Username ....

Password ....

Email ....

Password hint ....

Pin ....

Notes ....

....

Site Name ....

Site Address ....

Username ....

Password ....

Email ....

Password hint ....

Pin ....

Notes ....

....

Site Name ....

Site Address ....

Username ....

Password ....

Email ....

Password hint ....

Pin ....

Notes ....

....

S-T

U-V

W-X

Y-Z

Site Name ....
Site Address ....
Username ....
Password ....
Email ....
Password hint ....
Pin ....
Notes ....
....

Site Name ....
Site Address ....
Username ....
Password ....
Email ....
Password hint ....
Pin ....
Notes ....
....

Site Name ....
Site Address ....
Username ....
Password ....
Email ....
Password hint ....
Pin ....
Notes ....
....

Site Name ....

Site Address ....

Username ....

Password ....

Email ....

Password hint ....

Pin ....

Notes ....

....

Site Name ....

Site Address ....

Username ....

Password ....

Email ....

Password hint ....

Pin ....

Notes ....

....

Site Name ....

Site Address ....

Username ....

Password ....

Email ....

Password hint ....

Pin ....

Notes ....

....

S-T

U-V

W-X

Y-Z

Site Name ....
Site Address ....
Username ....
Password ....
Email ....
Password hint ....
Pin ....
Notes ....
....

Site Name ....
Site Address ....
Username ....
Password ....
Email ....
Password hint ....
Pin ....
Notes ....
....

Site Name ....
Site Address ....
Username ....
Password ....
Email ....
Password hint ....
Pin ....
Notes ....
....

Site Name ....
Site Address ....
Username ....
Password ....
Email ....
Password hint ....
Pin ....
Notes ....
....

Site Name ....
Site Address ....
Username ....
Password ....
Email ....
Password hint ....
Pin ....
Notes ....
....

Site Name ....
Site Address ....
Username ....
Password ....
Email ....
Password hint ....
Pin ....
Notes ....
....

S-T

U-V

W-X

Y-Z

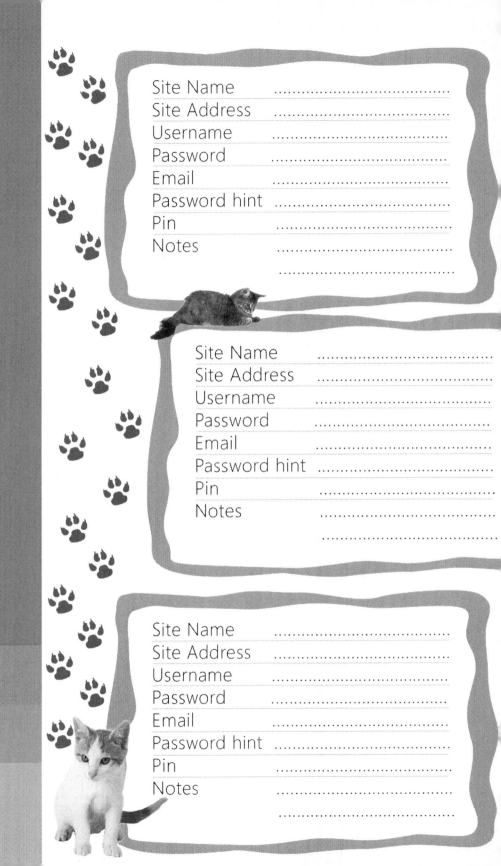

Site Name ....
Site Address ....
Username ....
Password ....
Email ....
Password hint ....
Pin ....
Notes ....
....

Site Name ....
Site Address ....
Username ....
Password ....
Email ....
Password hint ....
Pin ....
Notes ....
....

Site Name ....
Site Address ....
Username ....
Password ....
Email ....
Password hint ....
Pin ....
Notes ....
....

Site Name ....
Site Address ....
Username ....
Password ....
Email ....
Password hint ....
Pin ....
Notes ....
....

Site Name ....
Site Address ....
Username ....
Password ....
Email ....
Password hint ....
Pin ....
Notes ....
....

Site Name ....
Site Address ....
Username ....
Password ....
Email ....
Password hint ....
Pin ....
Notes ....
....

S-T

U-V

W-X

Y-Z

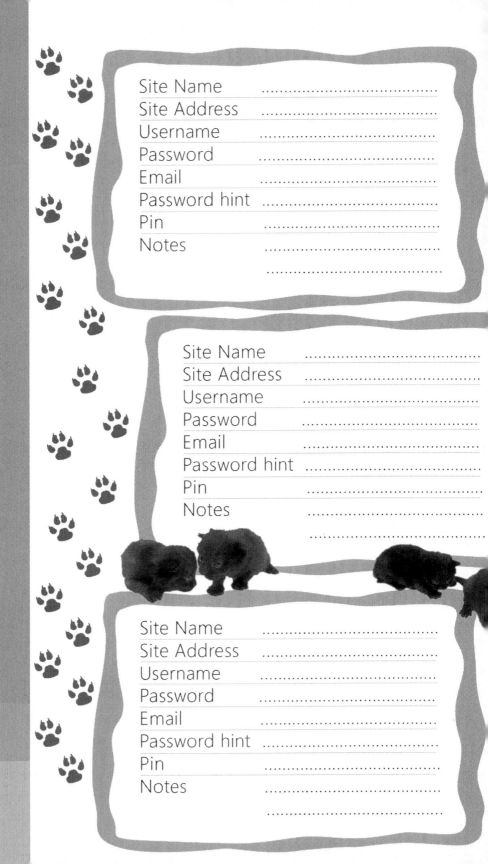

Site Name ....
Site Address ....
Username ....
Password ....
Email ....
Password hint ....
Pin ....
Notes ....
....

Site Name ....
Site Address ....
Username ....
Password ....
Email ....
Password hint ....
Pin ....
Notes ....
....

Site Name ....
Site Address ....
Username ....
Password ....
Email ....
Password hint ....
Pin ....
Notes ....
....

Site Name ....
Site Address ....
Username ....
Password ....
Email ....
Password hint ....
Pin ....
Notes ....
....

Site Name ....
Site Address ....
Username ....
Password ....
Email ....
Password hint ....
Pin ....
Notes ....
....

Site Name ....
Site Address ....
Username ....
Password ....
Email ....
Password hint ....
Pin ....
Notes ....
....

U-V

W-X

Y-Z

Site Name ....
Site Address ....
Username ....
Password ....
Email ....
Password hint ....
Pin ....
Notes ....
....

Site Name ....
Site Address ....
Username ....
Password ....
Email ....
Password hint ....
Pin ....
Notes ....
....

Site Name ....
Site Address ....
Username ....
Password ....
Email ....
Password hint ....
Pin ....
Notes ....
....

Site Name ....
Site Address ....
Username ....
Password ....
Email ....
Password hint ....
Pin ....
Notes ....
....

Site Name ....
Site Address ....
Username ....
Password ....
Email ....
Password hint ....
Pin ....
Notes ....
....

Site Name ....
Site Address ....
Username ....
Password ....
Email ....
Password hint ....
Pin ....
Notes ....
....

U-V

W-X

Y-Z

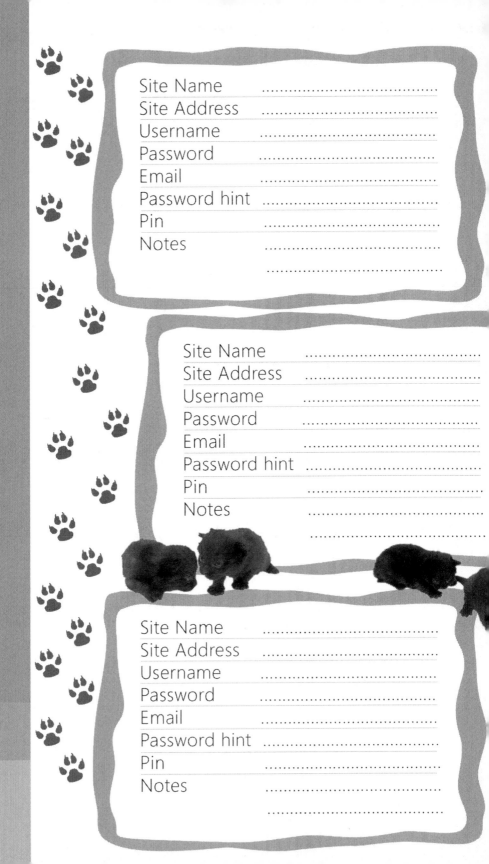

Site Name   ....
Site Address   ....
Username   ....
Password   ....
Email   ....
Password hint   ....
Pin   ....
Notes   ....
                 ....

Site Name   ....
Site Address   ....
Username   ....
Password   ....
Email   ....
Password hint   ....
Pin   ....
Notes   ....
                 ....

Site Name   ....
Site Address   ....
Username   ....
Password   ....
Email   ....
Password hint   ....
Pin   ....
Notes   ....
                 ....

Site Name   ....

Site Address   ....

Username   ....

Password   ....

Email   ....

Password hint   ....

Pin   ....

Notes   ....

....

Site Name   ....

Site Address   ....

Username   ....

Password   ....

Email   ....

Password hint   ....

Pin   ....

Notes   ....

....

Site Name   ....

Site Address   ....

Username   ....

Password   ....

Email   ....

Password hint   ....

Pin   ....

Notes   ....

....

U-V

W-X

Y-Z

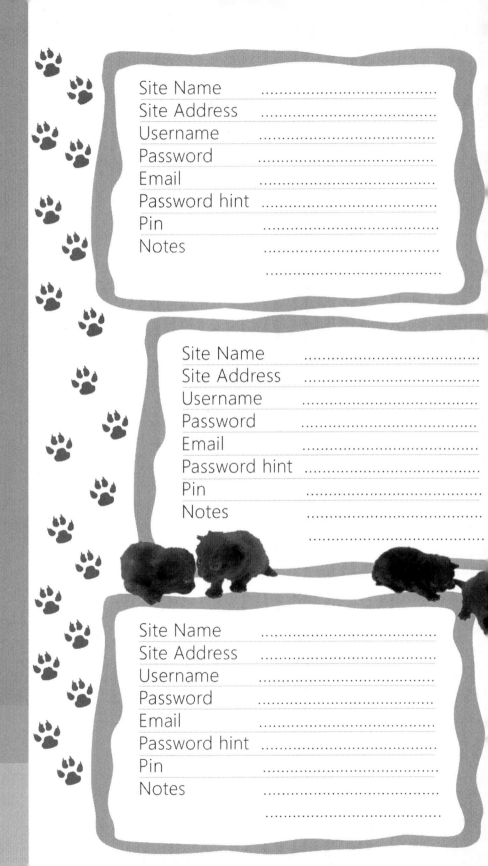

Site Name ....
Site Address ....
Username ....
Password ....
Email ....
Password hint ....
Pin ....
Notes ....
....

Site Name ....
Site Address ....
Username ....
Password ....
Email ....
Password hint ....
Pin ....
Notes ....
....

Site Name ....
Site Address ....
Username ....
Password ....
Email ....
Password hint ....
Pin ....
Notes ....
....

Site Name ....
Site Address ....
Username ....
Password ....
Email ....
Password hint ....
Pin ....
Notes ....
....

Site Name ....
Site Address ....
Username ....
Password ....
Email ....
Password hint ....
Pin ....
Notes ....
....

Site Name ....
Site Address ....
Username ....
Password ....
Email ....
Password hint ....
Pin ....
Notes ....
....

U-V

W-X

Y-Z

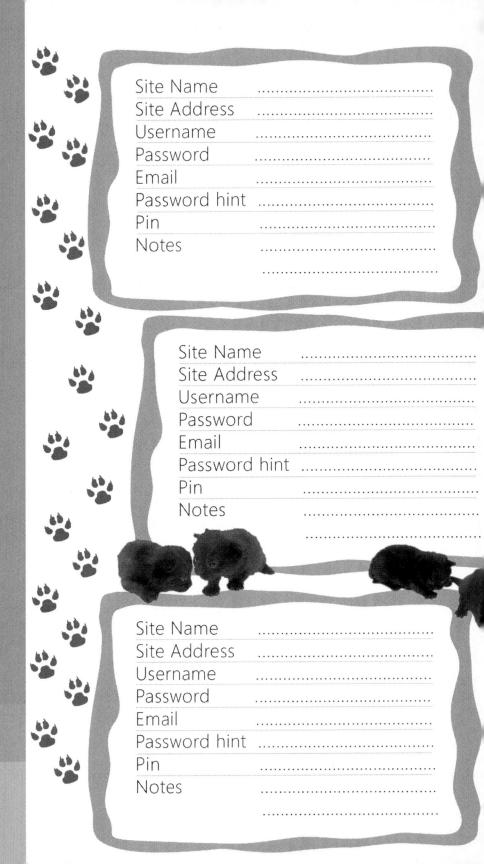

Site Name	
Site Address	
Username	
Password	
Email	
Password hint	
Pin	
Notes	

Site Name	
Site Address	
Username	
Password	
Email	
Password hint	
Pin	
Notes	

Site Name	
Site Address	
Username	
Password	
Email	
Password hint	
Pin	
Notes	

Site Name ....
Site Address ....
Username ....
Password ....
Email ....
Password hint ....
Pin ....
Notes ....
....

Site Name ....
Site Address ....
Username ....
Password ....
Email ....
Password hint ....
Pin ....
Notes ....
....

Site Name ....
Site Address ....
Username ....
Password ....
Email ....
Password hint ....
Pin ....
Notes ....
....

U-V

W-X

Y-Z

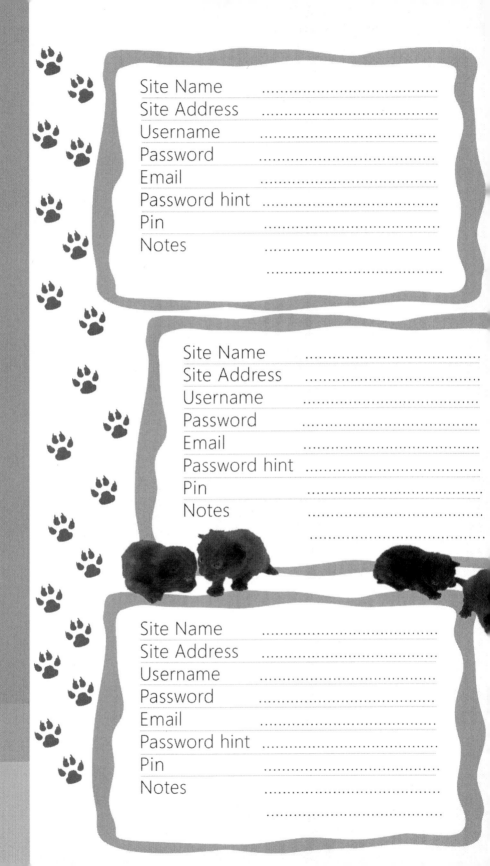

Site Name ....

Site Address ....

Username ....

Password ....

Email ....

Password hint ....

Pin ....

Notes ....

....

Site Name ....

Site Address ....

Username ....

Password ....

Email ....

Password hint ....

Pin ....

Notes ....

....

Site Name ....

Site Address ....

Username ....

Password ....

Email ....

Password hint ....

Pin ....

Notes ....

....

Site Name ....

Site Address ....

Username ....

Password ....

Email ....

Password hint ....

Pin ....

Notes ....

....

Site Name ....

Site Address ....

Username ....

Password ....

Email ....

Password hint ....

Pin ....

Notes ....

....

Site Name ....

Site Address ....

Username ....

Password ....

Email ....

Password hint ....

Pin ....

Notes ....

....

W-X

Y-Z

Site Name ....

Site Address ....

Username ....

Password ....

Email ....

Password hint ....

Pin ....

Notes ....

....

Site Name ....

Site Address ....

Username ....

Password ....

Email ....

Password hint ....

Pin ....

Notes ....

....

Site Name ....

Site Address ....

Username ....

Password ....

Email ....

Password hint ....

Pin ....

Notes ....

....

Site Name ....

Site Address ....

Username ....

Password ....

Email ....

Password hint ....

Pin ....

Notes ....

....

Site Name ....

Site Address ....

Username ....

Password ....

Email ....

Password hint ....

Pin ....

Notes ....

....

Site Name ....

Site Address ....

Username ....

Password ....

Email ....

Password hint ....

Pin ....

Notes ....

....

W-X

Y-Z

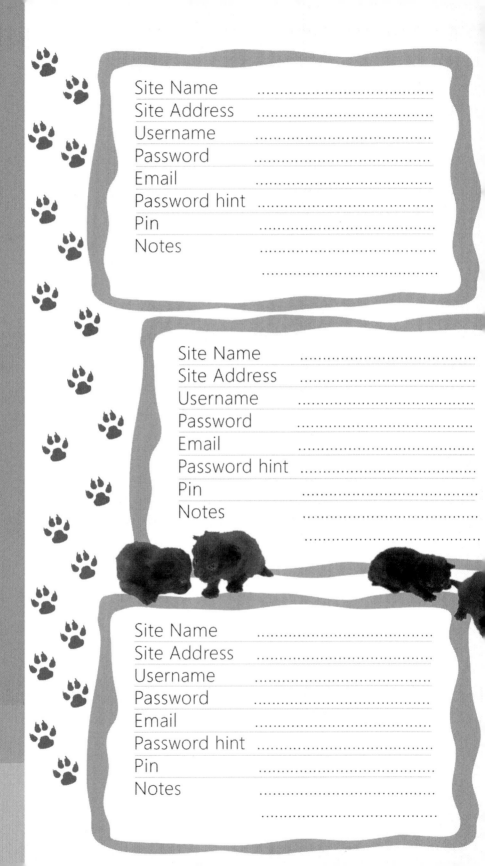

Site Name ....
Site Address ....
Username ....
Password ....
Email ....
Password hint ....
Pin ....
Notes ....
....

Site Name ....
Site Address ....
Username ....
Password ....
Email ....
Password hint ....
Pin ....
Notes ....
....

Site Name ....
Site Address ....
Username ....
Password ....
Email ....
Password hint ....
Pin ....
Notes ....
....

Site Name ....
Site Address ....
Username ....
Password ....
Email ....
Password hint ....
Pin ....
Notes ....
....

Site Name ....
Site Address ....
Username ....
Password ....
Email ....
Password hint ....
Pin ....
Notes ....
....

Site Name ....
Site Address ....
Username ....
Password ....
Email ....
Password hint ....
Pin ....
Notes ....
....

W-X

Y-Z

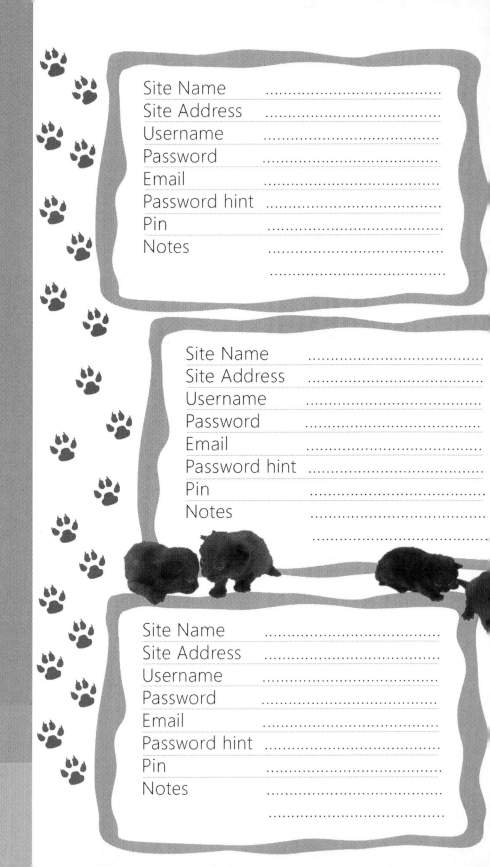

Site Name ....

Site Address ....

Username ....

Password ....

Email ....

Password hint ....

Pin ....

Notes ....

....

Site Name ....

Site Address ....

Username ....

Password ....

Email ....

Password hint ....

Pin ....

Notes ....

....

Site Name ....

Site Address ....

Username ....

Password ....

Email ....

Password hint ....

Pin ....

Notes ....

....

Site Name ....
Site Address ....
Username ....
Password ....
Email ....
Password hint ....
Pin ....
Notes ....
....

Site Name ....
Site Address ....
Username ....
Password ....
Email ....
Password hint ....
Pin ....
Notes ....
....

Site Name ....
Site Address ....
Username ....
Password ....
Email ....
Password hint ....
Pin ....
Notes ....
....

W-X

Y-Z

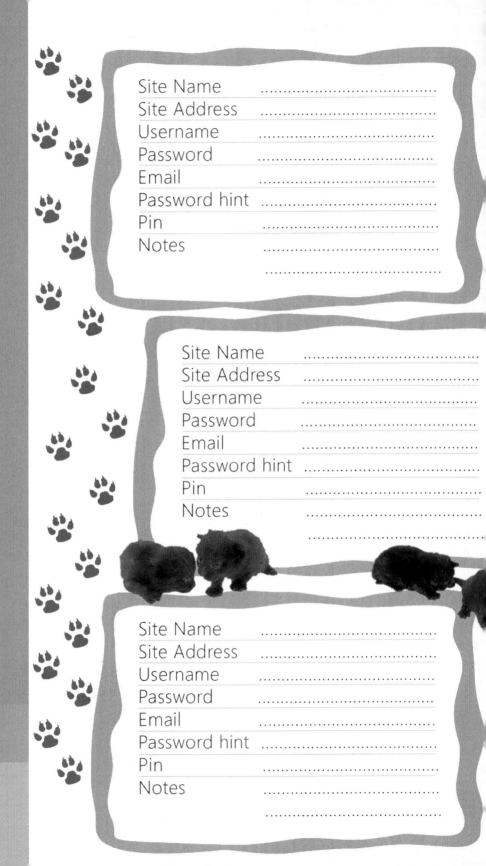

Site Name   ....
Site Address   ....
Username   ....
Password   ....
Email   ....
Password hint ....
Pin   ....
Notes   ....
     ....

Site Name   ....
Site Address   ....
Username   ....
Password   ....
Email   ....
Password hint ....
Pin   ....
Notes   ....
     ....

Site Name   ....
Site Address   ....
Username   ....
Password   ....
Email   ....
Password hint ....
Pin   ....
Notes   ....
     ....

Site Name ....
Site Address ....
Username ....
Password ....
Email ....
Password hint ....
Pin ....
Notes ....
....

Site Name ....
Site Address ....
Username ....
Password ....
Email ....
Password hint ....
Pin ....
Notes ....
....

Site Name ....
Site Address ....
Username ....
Password ....
Email ....
Password hint ....
Pin ....
Notes ....
....

W-X

Y-Z

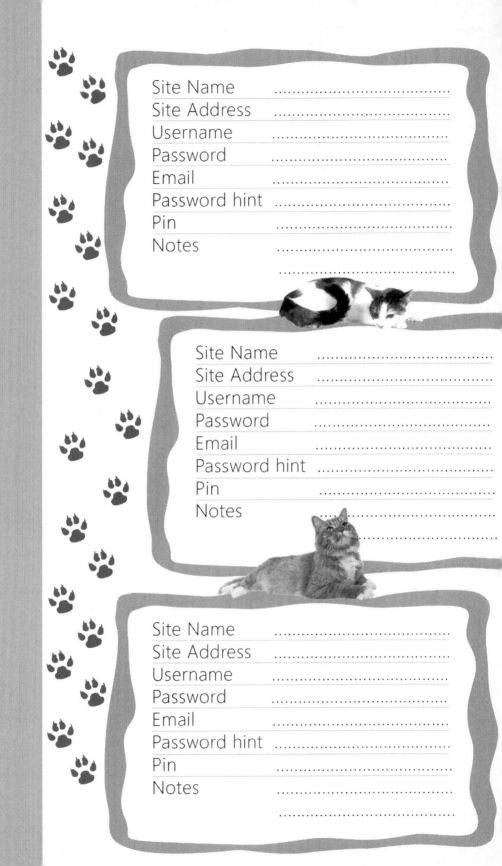

Site Name ....
Site Address ....
Username ....
Password ....
Email ....
Password hint ....
Pin ....
Notes ....
....

Site Name ....
Site Address ....
Username ....
Password ....
Email ....
Password hint ....
Pin ....
Notes ....
....

Site Name ....
Site Address ....
Username ....
Password ....
Email ....
Password hint ....
Pin ....
Notes ....
....

Site Name ....
Site Address ....
Username ....
Password ....
Email ....
Password hint ....
Pin ....
Notes ....
....

Site Name ....
Site Address ....
Username ....
Password ....
Email ....
Password hint ....
Pin ....
Notes ....
....

Site Name ....
Site Address ....
Username ....
Password ....
Email ....
Password hint ....
Pin ....
Notes ....
....

Y-Z

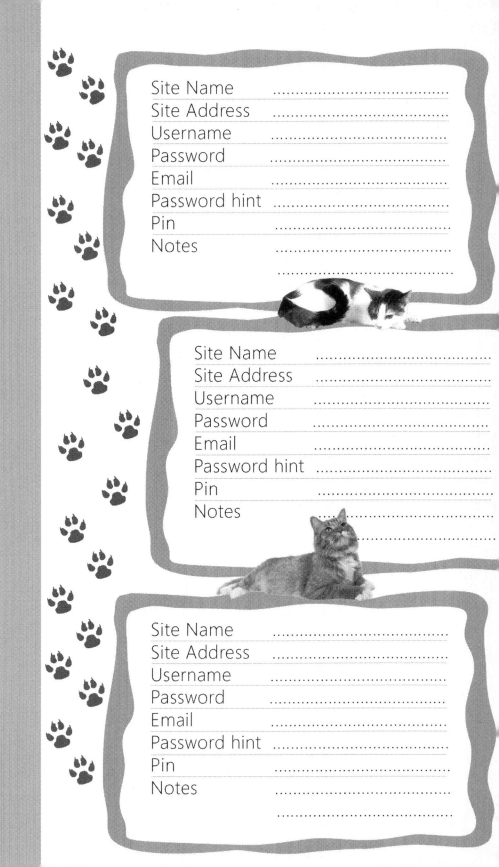

Site Name ....
Site Address ....
Username ....
Password ....
Email ....
Password hint ....
Pin ....
Notes ....
....

Site Name ....
Site Address ....
Username ....
Password ....
Email ....
Password hint ....
Pin ....
Notes ....
....

Site Name ....
Site Address ....
Username ....
Password ....
Email ....
Password hint ....
Pin ....
Notes ....
....

Site Name ....
Site Address ....
Username ....
Password ....
Email ....
Password hint ....
Pin ....
Notes ....
....

Site Name ....
Site Address ....
Username ....
Password ....
Email ....
Password hint ....
Pin ....
Notes ....
....

Site Name ....
Site Address ....
Username ....
Password ....
Email ....
Password hint ....
Pin ....
Notes ....
....

Y-Z

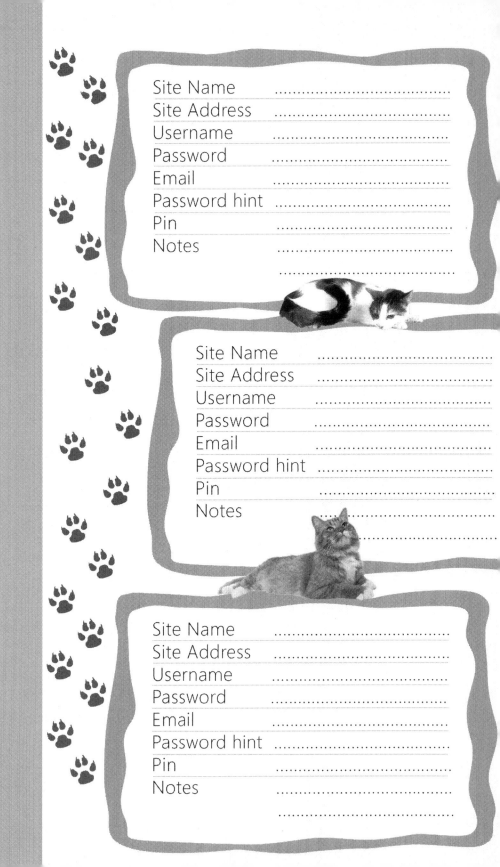

Site Name ....
Site Address ....
Username ....
Password ....
Email ....
Password hint ....
Pin ....
Notes ....

....

Site Name ....
Site Address ....
Username ....
Password ....
Email ....
Password hint ....
Pin ....
Notes ....

....

Site Name ....
Site Address ....
Username ....
Password ....
Email ....
Password hint ....
Pin ....
Notes ....

....

Site Name ....

Site Address ....

Username ....

Password ....

Email ....

Password hint ....

Pin ....

Notes ....

....

Site Name ....

Site Address ....

Username ....

Password ....

Email ....

Password hint ....

Pin ....

Notes ....

....

Site Name ....

Site Address ....

Username ....

Password ....

Email ....

Password hint ....

Pin ....

Notes ....

....

Y-Z

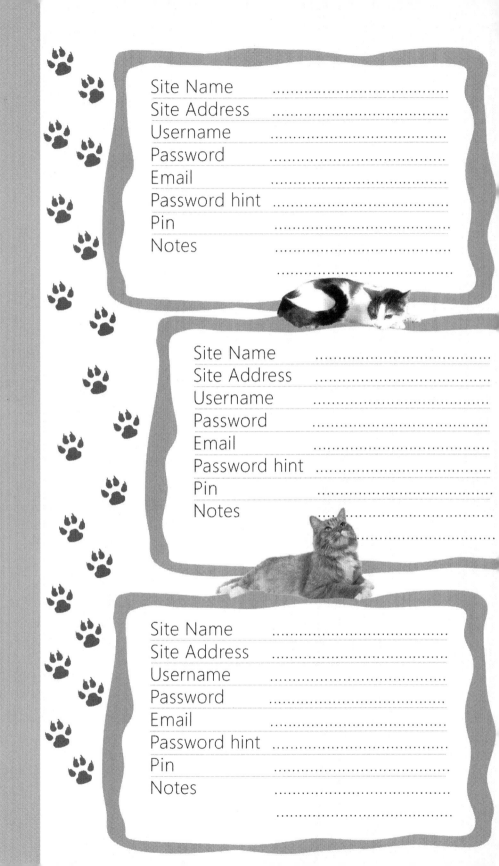

Site Name ....

Site Address ....

Username ....

Password ....

Email ....

Password hint ....

Pin ....

Notes ....

....

Site Name ....

Site Address ....

Username ....

Password ....

Email ....

Password hint ....

Pin ....

Notes ....

....

Site Name ....

Site Address ....

Username ....

Password ....

Email ....

Password hint ....

Pin ....

Notes ....

....

Site Name ....
Site Address ....
Username ....
Password ....
Email ....
Password hint ....
Pin ....
Notes ....
....

Site Name ....
Site Address ....
Username ....
Password ....
Email ....
Password hint ....
Pin ....
Notes ....
....

Site Name ....
Site Address ....
Username ....
Password ....
Email ....
Password hint ....
Pin ....
Notes ....
....

Y-Z

Internet Access Settings

Broadband Modem

Model
Serial number
Mac Address
Admin URL/IP Address
WAN IP Address
Username
Password
Notes

Router/ Wireless Access

*Useful if you need to reset your router or wireless access

Model
Serial Number
Default Username*
Default Password*
Your URL/IP Address
Your Username
Your Password
Notes

WAN Settings

Mac Address
Host Name
Domain Name
IP Address
Subnet Mask
Default Gateway
DNS
Notes

LAN
Settings

IP Address
Subnet Mask
DHCP Range
Notes

Wireless
Settings

SSID
(Wireless name)
Channel
Security Mode
WPA Shared Key
WEP Passphrase
Notes

Software
License number
Purchased on
Notes

Software
License number
Purchased on
Notes

Software
License number
Purchased on
Notes

Software
License number
Purchased on
Notes

Software
License number
Purchased on
Notes

Software
License number
Purchased on
Notes

Software
License number
Purchased on
Notes

Software
License number
Purchased on
Notes

Software
License number
Purchased on
Notes

Software
License number
Purchased on
Notes

Software
License number
Purchased on
Notes

Software
License number
Purchased on
Notes

Software
License number
Purchased on
Notes

Software
License number
Purchased on
Notes

Software
License number
Purchased on
Notes

Software
License number
Purchased on
Notes

Notes

Notes

Notes

A password book
disguised as a
photobook

P🐾WS-ITIVELY
PUPPIES

CERI CLARK

BOOKS IN THE SERIES...

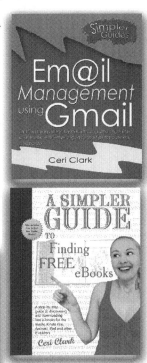

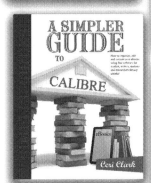

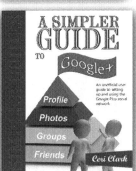

Made in United States
Orlando, FL
27 December 2021

12506654R00080